GW01246498

Original title:
A World Aglow

Author: Lan Donne
ISBN HARDBACK: 978-9908-52-029-2
ISBN PAPERBACK: 978-9908-52-030-8
ISBN EBOOK: 978-9908-52-031-5

Dreamscapes of Radiance

In twilight's embrace, where shadows dance,
Whispers of wonder, a fleeting chance.
Stars in the heavens begin to hum,
A symphony soft, inviting us to come.

Through valleys of gold, where sunlight spills,
Nature's sweet canvas, with vibrant thrills.
Petals of dreams in a gentle sway,
Invite us to wander, to drift away.

Mountains of silver touch skies of blue,
Illuminated pathways, ever anew.
Each step a story, each breath a song,
In these realms of light, we all belong.

Oceans of glimmer, secrets untold,
Waves wrap around us, tender and bold.
Carried on zephyrs, our spirits soar,
In this endless journey, forever explore.

With stardust in eyes, we awaken the night,
Basking in moments of pure delight.
Dreamscapes of radiance, alive and bright,
Where dreams intertwine with the whispers of light.

Brighter Than Before

In shadows deep, we found our way,
With every step, we chose to stay.
Through trials faced, we stood so tall,
Emerging strong, we won't let fall.

A spark ignites, a flame anew,
With every dawn, we push on through.
The past behind, with lessons learned,
A brighter path, our hearts now turned.

An Odyssey in Light

Across the seas of endless night,
We journey forth toward the light.
With every star, a path appears,
Guiding us through our hopes and fears.

Each step we take, the world expands,
We write our tale with open hands.
In distant lands where dreams unite,
Together strong, we glow so bright.

Kaleidoscope of Hope

In colors bold, our visions flow,
A dance of light in hearts aglow.
With each twist, the patterns change,
A vibrant world we can arrange.

We weave our dreams in threads of gold,
In every story waiting to be told.
Through every shade, through every hue,
A promise lies, forever true.

The Incandescent Heart

Within us beats a fiery core,
A rhythm strong, forevermore.
Through dark and light, it finds a way,
Embracing love in every sway.

The warmth it brings, a soothing balm,
In chaos still, we find our calm.
Our incandescent spirits soar,
For love will guide, forevermore.

The Ethereal Canvas

Whispers of color dance in the air,
Soft strokes of twilight blend with the flare.
Stars twinkle gently, a celestial sigh,
Beneath the vast veil of an infinite sky.

Moonlight spills silver on dreams yet to form,
Every shade cradling the night, safe and warm.
Canvas of cosmos, where thoughts intertwine,
Each hue tells a story, a fragment divine.

Fleeting moments captured, they shimmer and fade,
The artist of time in the quiet parade.
Echoes of brilliance in every dawn's gleam,
Nature paints softly, fulfilling each dream.

Beyond the Sunset

Crimson spills softly, the day's gentle end,
Horizons are kissed by colors that blend.
The sea whispers secrets, its waves rush to share,
Sanctuary beckons, an evening affair.

Golden reflections on water ignite,
Where shadows of night start to cradle the light.
Rays stretch like fingers, caressing the land,
As wishes take flight, like grains in the sand.

The stillness of twilight drapes over the hills,
Nature's sweet lullaby, a melody fills.
Footprints of sunlight now echo the past,
In the heart of the evening, such beauty amassed.

Spirals of Incandescence

In the dance of the night, bright spirals unfold,
Glimmers of light swirl in stories retold.
Whirling and twirling, they beckon the gaze,
A tapestry woven in luminous maze.

Flickers of firefly charm in the dark,
Each tiny glimmer, a flickering spark.
Infinite whispers on soft evening breeze,
A symphony sung beneath rustling trees.

Time bends with the glow, every heart takes a flight,
Caught in the magic, alive in the night.
In spirals of wonder, our spirits shall roam,
Guided by brilliance, we find our way home.

Brilliance of the Unknown

In shadows we wander, with hearts full of dreams,
Veiled in the silence, the universe gleams.
Questions like starlight encircle our fate,
As we reach through the dark, hoping to create.

Paths yet uncharted, where courage ignites,
In the brilliance of unknown, we soar to new heights.
Magic in possibility, whispers and sighs,
Crafting our story beneath endless skies.

With each step forward, the future unfolds,
A canvas of wonders in colors untold.
Embrace the uncertainty, let visions ignite,
For brilliance awaits in the depths of the night.

Glistening Dawn

The sun peeks over hills,
Soft colors start to blend.
Whispers of the new light,
Awakening the world.

Birds sing their cheerful songs,
As shadows disappear.
Morning dew on grass blades,
A fresh start to the day.

Clouds dance in the blue sky,
Fluffy and bright as dreams.
Nature's breath is gentle,
A calm that fills the heart.

The warmth of dawn unfolds,
In golden rays so pure.
Hope rises with the sun,
Chasing the night away.

Luminary Serenade

Stars twinkle in the night,
A symphony of light.
Each one tells a secret,
In the shadows, they glow.

Moonlight bathes the earth,
In a soft silvery hue.
Whispers of the cosmos,
Echo in quiet hearts.

Notes of a gentle breeze,
Carry tales from afar.
The night sings its lullabies,
To the world fast asleep.

Planets spin in their dance,
A waltz through the dark sky.
Each glimmer a reminder,
Of dreams yet to unfold.

As the night deepens deep,
Stars shine with such intent.
A serenade for souls,
Who wish upon their light.

Hope In Every Glint

Sunlight breaks through leaves,
Dancing on forest floors.
Every glint a promise,
Of brighter days ahead.

In the heart of the night,
A flicker shows the way.
Hope is found in shadows,
In the smallest of lights.

Raindrops on petals shine,
Nature's diamonds aglow.
They remind us to trust,
In the beauty of life.

Through trials and storms fierce,
We search for a soft glow.
Holding tight to our dreams,
In every spark we find.

With every dawn that breaks,
A new chance comes to play.
Hope lives in the glints,
Of courage and of love.

Glows of an Endless Sky

Twilight melts into night,
Colors blend and entwine.
The horizon whispers,
Secrets it keeps within.

Stars pierce the vast canvas,
In hues of silver dreams.
Galaxies spin above,
Infinite tales to tell.

Winds carry the echoes,
Of distant worlds gone by.
Each glow a connection,
To the wonders of time.

Clouds drift like soft shadows,
Beneath a watchful moon.
As night unfolds its cloak,
Mysteries come to play.

In this endless sky's dance,
Our souls find their own path.
We glow with the cosmos,
In this shared, sacred space.

Illuminated Paths

In the quiet woods they glow,
Footsteps light, the soft winds blow.
Guiding dreams through ancient trees,
Whispers echo on the breeze.

Each turn holds a story near,
Stars above, their light sincere.
Flickering hopes in shimmering night,
Reveal the truths that guide our sight.

With every step, the shadows play,
Dancing shadows softly sway.
Through the darkness, paths unfold,
Secrets of the brave and bold.

In deep silence, the heart can hear,
Stories told, crystal clear.
Embers of the day's delight,
Leads us onward, into light.

Nature's canvas, painted wide,
Courage found on every side.
Illuminated by the stars,
Love and wisdom heal our scars.

Celestial Abode

Above the clouds, a realm so bright,
Where dreams alight in silver light.
Celestial dances in the air,
Whispers of love and gentle care.

Moonlit paths twirl with grace,
Shooting stars leave their trace.
A tapestry of night's embrace,
The universe, our sacred space.

In the quiet of the heavenly glow,
Boundless peace, like rivers flow.
Hearts entwined in cosmic play,
Finding solace in the sway.

With each heartbeat, galaxies sing,
Eternal echoes rise and ring.
A celestial abode we seek,
In the silence, the spirits speak.

Endless beauty, pure and true,
In the stars, we find our due.
Journey's end, the soul's delight,
In celestial realms, we find our light.

Dance of the Fireflies

In twilight's glow, they twirl and weave,
A symphony that we believe.
Tiny lanterns in the dark,
Whispers close with every spark.

They flutter soft on gentle wings,
Nature's magic dances and sings.
Glowing trails through fields of green,
All around, the beauty seen.

Underneath the moon's embrace,
Stars above, they quicken pace.
Little hearts that soar and glide,
In the night, our dreams reside.

Catch a glimpse, a fleeting shine,
Moments lost in space and time.
A joyful dance beneath the night,
With each flicker, pure delight.

In harmony, they share their glow,
A ballet performed soft and slow.
The dance of fireflies, so divine,
Brings the magic, hearts align.

Echoes of the Sun

Golden rays on morning dew,
Whispers warm the world anew.
Echoes of the sun arise,
Painting blue across the skies.

Gentle warmth on every face,
Nature waking in its grace.
Each heartbeat syncs with the light,
Guiding us through day and night.

In the glow, we find our way,
Courage blooms with every ray.
Paths illuminated as we run,
Chasing dreams beneath the sun.

With every dawn, fresh tales unfold,
New beginnings to be told.
Echoes of laughter, smiles so bright,
Carry us into the night.

Together, we rise and shine,
In the warmth, our hearts entwine.
Echoes of the sun we feel,
In every moment, love is real.

The Light Within

In shadows deep where whispers dwell,
A flicker glows, a silent bell.
Each heart a spark, a flame reborn,
Guiding us through the dark forlorn.

Beneath the weight of doubt and fear,
The light within breaks, ever clear.
A beacon bright in winter's fight,
It fuels the soul, ignites the night.

Through storms that rage and tempests howl,
The inner fire begins to growl.
With every breath, it claims its throne,
In quiet strength, we're not alone.

Awake, arise, let courage soar,
With each heartbeat, we yearn for more.
The path may twist, but still we seek,
The light within makes us unique.

In unity, we stand as one,
Embracing light till day is done.
Together we will dance and sing,
For inside us lies everything.

Aurora of Promises

A canvas brushed with hues of dawn,
Awakening dreams, the night is gone.
The sky ignites in fiery grace,
An aurora paints the vast, open space.

Whispers of hope in every ray,
As night's shadows fade away.
Promises gleam in golden light,
A tapestry woven, pure and bright.

Each color sings of tales untold,
Of hearts ignited, of spirits bold.
The horizon gleams with future's kiss,
In every dawn, a chance for bliss.

Let every moment, pure and clear,
Guide us forward, banish fear.
With every sunrise, dreams take flight,
In the embrace of morning light.

In this symphony, we find our way,
A harmony that holds the day.
The aurora whispers, sweet and fair,
In every promise, love lays bare.

Shining Through the Veil of Time

Time flows like rivers, swift and wide,
Carrying moments on its tide.
Yet through its veil, a light still gleams,
Revealing fragments of our dreams.

Each heartbeat echoes from the past,
Memories linger, shadows cast.
But in the twilight, truth reveals,
A shine that every soul appeals.

The sands of time may slip away,
Yet hope remains, a bright array.
In every glance, a story sighs,
Shining through where spirit lies.

We gather strength from all that's flown,
With courage forged and seeds well sown.
Even as the years unwind,
A radiant truth awakens, aligned.

So when the night begins to fall,
We heed the light, we heed the call.
For in the darkness, stars will chime,
Shining through the veil of time.

Iridescent Reflections

In puddles vast, the world appears,
A mirror of hopes, a dance of fears.
Iridescent waves in colors blend,
Each ripple whispers, stories send.

Through the glassy sheen, we see our past,
Moments captured, fleeting, fast.
Yet through the chaos, beauty grows,
A reminder of all that life bestows.

Like prisms bending in soft light,
Our truths emerge, shining bright.
In every shade, a lesson learned,
In every turn, our spirit burned.

With every glance, a chance to find,
The threads of love that intertwine.
Together in this dance we tread,
With iridescent dreams we've bred.

So let us gaze into the clear,
Embrace the light, discard the fear.
For in those waves, we find our song,
In iridescent reflections, we belong.

Celestial Dances

In the vast expanse of night,
Stars twirl in a cosmic flight.
Galaxies spin with grace and glow,
As the universe puts on a show.

Planets waltz, their paths entwined,
Celestial rhythms, perfectly timed.
Comets race with fiery tails,
In the dark where beauty prevails.

Nebulas bloom in colors bright,
Painting the canvas of the night.
Each flicker tells a tale of old,
In the silence, whispers unfold.

Stardust drifts on gentle breeze,
Carrying secrets through the trees.
The moon smiles, a watchful friend,
Guiding each dance, without end.

So lift your eyes, let dreams take flight,
Join the dance of stars tonight.
In the harmony of the skies,
Hope and wonder ever rise.

Starlit Murmurs

Underneath a sky so wide,
Whispers of the night abide.
Stars exchange their gentle sighs,
Echoes of the universe's ties.

Moonbeams pass soft rays around,
In this hush, magic is found.
Each twinkle shares a secret scheme,
In the dark, they softly gleam.

The cosmos hums a lullaby,
Drawing hearts to dream and fly.
Pulsars send a steady beat,
A melody both light and sweet.

Galactic winds gracefully weave,
Stories held in webs that cleave.
In the silence, wonders stir,
Carried softly, a starlit purr.

So lean in close and hear the sound,
Of the universe spinning round.
In every shimmer, every sigh,
Lives the essence of the sky.

The Enchanted Glow

In twilight's embrace, shadows dance,
Nature awakens in a trance.
Fireflies flicker, their spells so sweet,
Painting the dusk where dreams can meet.

Moonlight drapes the world in silk,
A soft caress, like warm milk.
Petals open, kissed by dew,
In the garden, magic brews.

Whispers rise from the ancient trees,
A serenade on the evening breeze.
The air is thick with fragrant balm,
Nature's pulse beats soft and calm.

Hidden paths under stellar skies,
Lead to wonders, where beauty lies.
Each twinkling light a secret shared,
In the glow, we find we're cared.

So linger long in this twilight show,
Let your heart in silence flow.
For in the night's enchanted hue,
Magic awaits, just for you.

Symphony of Shimmers

In the garden, the stars align,
Creating a symphony divine.
Each glitter, a note in the air,
A melody rich beyond compare.

Dewdrops twinkle on the grass,
Harmonies of light amassed.
Gentle breezes carry the song,
In the night where dreams belong.

Whirls of silver, splashes of gold,
Stories of the night unfold.
The cosmos sings, a vibrant choir,
With every star, hearts lift higher.

Echoes of the cosmos play,
Guiding souls that roam astray.
Let the music fill your heart,
In this dance, we're never apart.

So close your eyes, let visions soar,
Join the chorus forevermore.
In the symphony of shimmers bright,
Find your place in the cosmic night.

Murmurs of the Dawn

Whispers in the morning light,
A gentle brush of golden hue.
Nature wakes with soft delight,
As dreams fade from the view.

Birds begin their tender calls,
The world awakens, fresh and bright.
New possibilities enthrall,
Underneath the sky's first light.

The dew-kissed grass sparkles fine,
Beneath the sun's embrace we stand.
Time flows as a gentle line,
Marking moments, oh so grand.

Every shadow fades away,
Chasing darkness, bold and strong.
Hope arises with the day,
In this melody, we belong.

As horizons start to glow,
Life ignites in vibrant hues.
In the dawn, our spirits flow,
Murmurs dance in morning dues.

Firelight Revelations

Crackling embers on the stone,
Casting warmth in twilight's dance.
Stories linger, hearts have grown,
Around the fire, we take a chance.

Faces flicker, shadows play,
Whispers echo, dreams ignite.
In the stillness, night turns sway,
Glowing truths in shared delight.

Years of laughter, tears, and fears,
A tapestry we weave so tight.
Memories etched through all the years,
In the fire's tender light.

Voices blend in soft refrain,
As the night unfolds its grace.
Each revelation born of pain,
Finds solace in this sacred space.

Chasing shadows with our tales,
Through the flames, our spirits soar.
In the warmth, the heart prevails,
Firelight's gift forevermore.

Journey Through Radiance

Beneath the arch of sapphire skies,
A path unfolds, inviting dreams.
With every step, the spirit flies,
In sunlight's glow, we're not what seems.

Fields of amber stretch so wide,
Whispers of promise in the breeze.
Adventure calls, we do not hide,
In every moment, wander with ease.

Mountains rise with regal grace,
Challenging the heart and soul.
With courage found, we find our place,
In every climb, we feel more whole.

Rivers sing a timeless song,
Binding land and heart in flow.
As we tread where hopes belong,
Through radiance, we come to know.

Every corner holds a truth,
A lesson wrapped in nature's art.
In this journey, reclaim your youth,
Radiance ignites every heart.

Sparks of Destiny

In the quiet of the night,
Stars awaken, bright and clear.
Fates align, a cosmic sight,
Whispers of what's drawing near.

Every moment holds a spark,
Illuminating paths we tread.
With every light, a brand-new arc,
Guiding where our hearts are led.

Dreams ignite like flames anew,
As we chase what lies ahead.
In the stillness, hope breaks through,
Sparks of destiny, gently spread.

Fear may linger, shadows cast,
But courage flares in heart's embrace.
In the future's glow, we cast,
A tapestry of time and space.

Embrace the sparks that come your way,
They light the darkness, carve a path.
With every choice, a chance to sway,
To dance with fate's sweet aftermath.

Twilight's Embrace

As the sun sinks low, a soft glow,
Whispers of night begin to flow.
Stars awaken, shimmering bright,
In twilight's arms, the world feels right.

Gentle shadows dance on the ground,
In the silence, peace is found.
Moonlight drapes the earth in grace,
Wrapped in twilight's warm embrace.

Colors bleed in dusky hue,
Crickets serenade the view.
A canvas painted dark and light,
As day surrenders to the night.

Dreams take flight on the evening breeze,
Carried softly through the trees.
In this moment, hearts align,
In twilight's glow, all is divine.

The world grows still, a sacred pause,
Nature rests without applause.
In the twilight, calm persists,
A gentle hush, a lover's tryst.

Sparkling Dreams

In the night, dreams start to gleam,
Like stars that wink, they softly beam.
Promises whispered, secrets told,
In sparkling realms, where hearts unfold.

Silver threads weave through the air,
Crafting wishes with tender care.
Each flicker holds a story dear,
In the magic, we lose our fear.

Clouds become castles, drifting high,
On wings of hope, we learn to fly.
Every twinkle calls our name,
In sparkling dreams, we'll find our flame.

A symphony of light and sound,
In this wonderland, we're unbound.
With every heartbeat, we ignite,
Chasing visions into the night.

Awake or dream, we seek the same,
In the depths, we play our game.
Through sparkling dreams, we find the way,
To brighter tomorrows, come what may.

Colors of the Heart

In gentle strokes, the canvas bleeds,
A tapestry of hopes and needs.
Crimson whispers, sapphire sighs,
In colors of the heart, love flies.

Golden rays of morning's hue,
Brush the sky with shades so true.
Lavender thoughts in twilight's hold,
Stories of life and love retold.

Vivid dreams in emerald realms,
Where passion and joy overwhelm.
Beneath the surface, shadows play,
In colors bright, we find our way.

Every heartbeat paints a scene,
In colors vibrant, wild, serene.
Mixing laughter with the pain,
In the palette, we all remain.

As the colors blend and sway,
They tell the tale of every day.
In the hues, our spirits dance,
Embracing life's sweet, fleeting chance.

Shimmering Reflections

In quiet pools, the light does play,
Reflecting dreams in bright array.
Every ripple tells a tale,
Of love and hopes that never pale.

Mirrored skies in silver sheen,
Capture moments, softly seen.
Each reflection, a gentle sigh,
Beneath the stars, where wishes lie.

The water's edge, a secret place,
Where time stands still in soft embrace.
With every glance, new worlds ignite,
In shimmering views, pure delight.

The night unfolds its velvet cloak,
As whispers bloom and shadows spoke.
In mirrored depths, our hearts align,
Finding solace, purely divine.

A dance of light, a poet's dream,
In shimmering reflections, we gleam.
Guided by the moon's soft glow,
In these moments, love will flow.

Twilight's Luster

The sun dips low in the pale sky,
Silhouettes dance as shadows sigh.
Colors blend, a soft embrace,
Whispers linger, time slows its pace.

Stars awake in the woven night,
Dreams are born in the fading light.
Night's cool breath on a gentle breeze,
Nature sighs, and the world feels at ease.

Crickets sing in a rhythmic tune,
While the glow of dusk sways to the moon.
Stars twinkle like secrets untold,
In twilight's grasp, the magic unfolds.

The horizon drinks the last of day,
A canvas painted in shades of gray.
As silence falls, the night takes the floor,
Twilight's luster, we all adore.

With every heartbeat, calm descends,
In twilight's arms, worry ends.
Moments linger, they softly last,
In the glow where light meets the past.

The Charm of Dusk

Dusk descends with a gentle grace,
Inviting thoughts to a slower pace.
Clouds blush softly in vibrant hues,
In this moment, the world feels new.

The breeze carries whispers of dreams,
Reflecting life in its flowing streams.
Golden rays fading into night,
Filling hearts with soft delight.

Birds return to their cozy nests,
As day retreats and night behests.
The moon peeks through a silver veil,
Tales of twilight begin to sail.

Stars shimmer like gleaming dew,
Each one a wish, each one a clue.
In the charm of dusk, we find our way,
A golden promise of a brand new day.

So let us pause, and breathe it in,
The soothing peace where dreams begin.
In twilight's glow, our spirits soar,
Holding tight to the heart's allure.

Glows of Solitude

In solitude's quiet embrace,
I find a space, a sacred place.
Soft glows flicker, a tender light,
Guiding thoughts into the night.

Moments drift on a gentle breeze,
Rustling leaves, a rustle of ease.
Stars blink softly, a comforting sign,
In solitude, the heart aligns.

Time stretches out in sweet reprieve,
In glows of solitude, we believe.
Each thought a whisper, a gentle sway,
In the silence, we find our way.

The world outside fades to a hum,
As peace within becomes a drum.
Illuminated by dreams untold,
In solitude, our spirits unfold.

With every breath, embrace the calm,
Let the heart sing its soothing psalm.
In the glow of quiet's embrace,
Find your strength, find your place.

Illuminated Journeys

Journeys unfold like the morning sun,
With every heartbeat, a new one begun.
Paths illuminated, guiding our way,
In the dance of light, we find our play.

With every step, stories take flight,
Whispers of hope in the crisp daylight.
Mountains rise, valleys stretch wide,
In luminous trails, we learn to glide.

Dreams weave through the tapestry bright,
Colors merging in the soft twilight.
Footsteps imprinted on the sands of time,
Eager hearts with a rhythm and rhyme.

Through the shadows, we boldly tread,
With courage ignited and worries shed.
In our souls, an unwavering spark,
Illuminated journeys, we embark.

With the stars as guides, we won't be lost,
Embracing the journey, whatever the cost.
Every moment blessed, every road a song,
In illuminated paths, we all belong.

Halo of Serenity

In the hush of twilight's glow,
Soft whispers dance where breezes flow.
Petals drift on gentle streams,
Wrapped in the calm of tranquil dreams.

Moonlight casts its silver lace,
Cradling night in a warm embrace.
Stars awaken in the sky,
Guiding hearts that long to fly.

Stillness cradles every sigh,
Lifting spirits ever high.
Peace resides where shadows fall,
In this serene and sacred hall.

Nature sings a lullaby,
While the world drifts softly by.
Each heartbeat finds its gentle rest,
In a haven that feels blessed.

Here, all worries fade away,
As night transforms the end of day.
A halo glows within the mind,
Revealing calm we long to find.

Cascading Brilliance

Golden rays through branches seep,
Awakening the earth from sleep.
Colors burst in dazzling hues,
Nature's canvas paints the views.

Leaves shimmer in the sunlit air,
Whispers of a breeze everywhere.
The river sparkles with delight,
Merging earth and sky so bright.

Mountains echo vibrant calls,
As waterfalls meet the gentle falls.
Every moment, wonder sparks,
In the beauty of nature's marks.

With every step, new paths arise,
Each glance reveals a sweet surprise.
Life's dance flows like the streams,
Floating softly on shared dreams.

Cascading brilliance surrounds all,
In this realm where hearts enthrall.
Here the world is alive and free,
In harmony, you and me.

Flickering Memories

Echoes linger in the air,
Whispers of a time laid bare.
Flickering lights in fading days,
Illuminate forgotten ways.

Moments caught like fireflies,
Dancing softly 'neath the skies.
Each smile shared, a fleeting glance,
Time's sweet waltz, an endless dance.

In the corners of the mind,
Treasured fragments, love entwined.
Memories like shadows play,
Chasing sunlight from the day.

Hold them tight, let silence gleam,
Glimmers from a cherished dream.
In nostalgia's warm embrace,
Flickering lights find their place.

Time may fade, but hearts remain,
Whispering softly through the pain.
Clinging close to what we know,
Flickering memories, softly glow.

Dreams in Technicolor

In vivid hues, the visions bloom,
Painting life within the room.
A tapestry of hopes unfurled,
Bringing magic to the world.

Every shade a story tells,
Of laughter shared and ringing bells.
Imaginations take their flight,
In the brilliant canvas of the night.

Stars twinkle in brilliant swirls,
As dreams awaken, dance, and twirl.
All the colors swirl and blend,
In a realm where time transcends.

Beyond the bounds of black and white,
Where shadows fade and hearts take flight.
A symphony of sights and sounds,
In technicolor joy resounds.

As dawn breaks, the hues may fade,
But in our hearts, the dreams are made.
Forever vivid, bright, and clear,
In every dream, we hold dear.

Flickering Solstice

The sun dips low, a golden hue,
Whispers of dusk, a gentle brew.
Stars awaken in the cool night's air,
Flickers of light, beyond compare.

The shadows dance on the forest floor,
Nature's canvas, an open door.
Moonbeams weave through the ancient trees,
A symphony played by the evening breeze.

As twilight breathes, the world slows down,
A moment captured, without a frown.
In the stillness, time stands still,
A magic woven, as dreams fulfill.

The night embraces with tender grace,
In the vast sky, we find our place.
A flicker here, a shimmer there,
Life's fleeting beauty, beyond compare.

Shimmering Essence

Under the stars, that soft glow,
Whispers of secrets, we long to know.
Each breath a moment, each gaze a spark,
In the stillness, we leave our mark.

The rivers shimmer, a silver thread,
Guiding our hearts where dreams are bred.
In every ripple, a story unfolds,
Of love and loss, of courage bold.

Through fields of wildflowers, we wander free,
Nature's essence, a jubilee.
Petals whisper tales in the breeze,
We chase the light beneath the trees.

In moonlit corners where shadows play,
We gather pauses in the fray.
Each sparkling moment, a glimpse divine,
In the tapestry of life, we intertwine.

The Light That Binds

In the tapestry of night, we find a thread,
A glowing bond, where words are said.
The light that binds, a sacred glow,
Through laughter and tears, together we grow.

Reflections shimmer in your gaze,
A beacon of hope through life's maze.
In the silence shared, our spirits soar,
The light connects us, forevermore.

Through open hearts and open skies,
In every moment, true love lies.
With hands entwined, we walk as one,
In the dance of life, the journey's fun.

As dawn breaks forth, a promise clear,
The light that binds will always near.
In every shadow and every light,
Together we shine, through day and night.

Chasing Firefly Visions

Beneath the stars, the night unfolds,
With whispers soft and stories told.
We chase the fireflies, glowing bright,
In a magical world, pure delight.

Wings of wonder drift in the air,
Each tiny flicker, a dream laid bare.
Through fields of dreams, our laughter flows,
In every dance, a mystery grows.

Together we wander under the sky,
With open hearts, we learn to fly.
In the chase for light, we find our way,
Illuminated paths, come what may.

As time slips softly like grains of sand,
Our firefly visions, hand in hand.
In the night's embrace, we'll always roam,
Chasing the magic that leads us home.

Glistening Visions

In the twilight, dreams arise,
Shimmering whispers, soft as sighs.
Colors dance in the fading light,
Crafting visions, pure and bright.

Through the shadows, secrets bloom,
A canvas painted, dispelling gloom.
Stars awaken, twinkling dear,
Guiding hearts, silencing fear.

Glistening paths unfold anew,
Each step forward, bold and true.
Embrace the magic, let it show,
In every moment, let love grow.

Life's a journey, wild and free,
Glistening visions call to me.
With open arms, I shall explore,
The realms of wonder, forevermore.

The Poetic Light

In the dawn, a gentle glow,
Whispers of the day to flow.
Words like petals, soft and fair,
Breathe the moment, fill the air.

Each line crafted, heart fulfilled,
In silence, all my dreams distilled.
Ink and paper, dance in tune,
Underneath the silver moon.

Through valleys low and mountains high,
The poetic light will never die.
It guides the lost, it warms the cold,
A treasure more than gems or gold.

In every verse, a world awaits,
A symphony that captivates.
Let it linger, let it ignite,
The soulful spark, the poetic light.

A Glimpse of Wonder

In the garden, colors play,
Nature's canvas bright and gay.
Butterflies flutter on the breeze,
With every bloom, my heart it frees.

A whispering stream, soft and clear,
Carries tales for those who hear.
Rustling leaves and gentle sighs,
Invite the dreams that never die.

The sun dips low, the sky aglow,
Painting wonders we come to know.
In fleeting moments, beauty speaks,
Glimmers of magic, whispered tweaks.

A glimpse of wonder, pure delight,
Awakens joy, ignites the night.
Hold it close, in heart and mind,
A treasure trove of joy to find.

Flickering Hope

In the darkness, a candle's flame,
Flickering softly, calling your name.
Through the shadows, it dances bright,
A beacon of warmth, a guiding light.

Whispers of hope in silent air,
Embracing hearts, healing despair.
Each tiny spark, a promise new,
A reminder that dreams can come true.

Storms may rage and skies may grey,
Yet flickering hope will lead the way.
With every breath, I hold it tight,
A flame within, igniting the night.

No matter how far the journey goes,
Flickering hope forever grows.
In the chaos, it stands alone,
A gentle pulse, a steadfast tone.

The Radiant Pulse

In the heart of night, it beats,
A glow that cannot hide.
Whispers of the cosmos sing,
In rhythms that abide.

Stars pulse in vibrant hues,
Each spark a tale to tell.
Waves of warmth and fire dance,
In the quiet, they dwell.

Through shadows, light reveals,
The secrets that we chase.
In every fleeting moment,
We find our destined place.

Awakening the dawn,
With colors rich and bright.
The world begins to shimmer,
In the embrace of light.

The pulse of life persists,
In each beat, dreams arise.
We follow where it leads us,
To the vast, open skies.

Flicker of Eternity

Time weaves a silent thread,
In moments soft and sweet.
A flicker catches breath,
Of past and future meet.

In the dance of shadows cast,
Elders whisper low.
Echoes of the ages,
In twilight's gentle glow.

Each flicker holds a story,
Of love, of loss, of gain.
In every fleeting heartbeat,
Life's lessons still remain.

The stars blink knowingly,
In constellations old.
They guide the lost wanderers,
With tales of courage bold.

A flicker in the darkness,
Can light a path anew.
In the embrace of eternity,
Our spirits will break through.

Breaths of Starlight

The night exhales softly,
In breaths of starlight bright.
Each twinkle, an invitation,
To dance in the cool night.

Winds carry ancient stories,
From galaxies afar.
In every whispered secret,
We find just who we are.

The moon cradles the silence,
In her glowing embrace.
With each pulse of the heavens,
We taste the endless space.

Breaths of light entwine us,
In a tapestry divine.
Every flicker a reminder,
Of love that will not decline.

In shadows we find hope,
In darkness, pure delight.
Breaths of starlight guide us,
Through the stillness of the night.

A Tapestry of Light

Threads of gold and silver,
Intertwine and weave.
A tapestry of moments,
In which we dare believe.

Colors of our laughter,
And hues of joy and pain.
In the fabric of existence,
We find our hearts remain.

A gentle hand to follow,
As we dance through the dark.
The stitches hold us closer,
Each one, a sacred mark.

With patterns ever shifting,
The light begins to show.
In this rich creation,
We find the path to grow.

A tapestry of light,
Embroidered by our dreams.
We gather in connection,
As one, or so it seems.

Gleaming Threads of Tomorrow

In the dawn's gentle hue,
Hope begins to unfold,
Dreams like whispers on breeze,
A tapestry of gold.

Each step we take with care,
We weave the future bright,
Threads of courage entwined,
In the fabric of light.

Through valleys of shadow,
We search for the spark,
With faith as our compass,
We ignite the dark.

Moments become patterns,
In this quest we pursue,
A journey shared together,
With visions anew.

So we gather our dreams,
And stitch them with love,
In the gleaming threads,
The tomorrow we dream of.

Nature's Canvas Awash in Light

Beneath the wide blue sky,
Colors dance and play,
Each leaf a brushstroke bright,
In nature's grand display.

Mountains stand like giants,
Whispers in the breeze,
Rivers sing their stories,
Through valleys and through trees.

Sunsets paint the horizon,
With strokes of fiery gold,
A masterpiece unfolding,
Every tale retold.

Flowers bloom like laughter,
In hues that catch the eye,
Nature's art abundant,
A feast for heart and sky.

So let us wander free,
In this vibrant delight,
For every step a canvas,
Awash in golden light.

Lighthouses of the Soul

In tempest's wild embrace,
Stand the lighthouses tall,
Guiding lost ships with hope,
When shadows start to fall.

With beams of warmth and truth,
They pierce the cloudy night,
Illuminating paths,
To restore our inner sight.

Through storms of doubt and fear,
These towers never sway,
Their steadfast keeps the flame,
A beacon on our way.

As sailors seek their shore,
We search for our own peace,
In lighthouses of love,
Our burdens start to cease.

So let us hold them dear,
For they whisper the whole,
In every heart a lighthouse,
A comfort for the soul.

The Artist's Illumination

With every stroke of brush,
An echo of the heart,
Colors swirl and blend,
In a dance of art.

Canvas waits in stillness,
For dreams to take their flight,
In shadows and in light,
The artist's pure delight.

In quiet contemplation,
Imaginations bloom,
Whispers of creation,
Dispelling all the gloom.

Each line a quiet story,
Each hue a vivid thought,
A journey of expression,
In every piece they've brought.

So let the muse awaken,
And let your heart unfold,
For in the artist's vision,
A world of wonders told.

The Glow of Distant Horizons

Upon the ridge, the sun will rise,
Casting gold across the skies.
Mountains bathed in morning light,
Whispers of the coming night.

A promise waits in every hue,
As day unfolds its canvas new.
Soft shadows stretch, the night departs,
Awakening the dreaming hearts.

Waves of color, bold and bright,
Painting stories of the night.
A tapestry of dusk and dawn,
Where hopes are cherished, dreams are drawn.

Paths that wind through fields of grace,
Guided by the stars' embrace.
Every step, a tale untold,
A journey where the brave are bold.

So chase the glow, let spirits soar,
The horizon calls, forevermore.
In every sunset, a new start,
As light and shadow play their part.

Where Starlight Dances

In midnight's cloak, the stars awake,
Each one a wish, a silent ache.
They shimmer soft in cosmic grace,
A dance of light in endless space.

Silver trails weave tales of old,
Of ancient dreams and secrets bold.
With every twinkle, stories bloom,
Illuminating the encroaching gloom.

Beneath this sky, hearts intertwine,
In the hush, your hand in mine.
We spin through time, where shadows play,
In starlit realms, we lose our way.

Whispers caught in the cool night air,
As moonlight cloaks us with its flare.
Here in the magic, we find our song,
In celestial depths, we both belong.

So let us dance under this vast dome,
In the embrace of the stars, our home.
For in this moment, all is right,
Where starlight dances, love ignites.

Illuminated Paths

Beneath the trees, where shadows creep,
Illuminated paths begin to leap.
Guided by the soft, glowing fair,
Leading souls with tender care.

The lanterns sway in gentle breeze,
Whispering secrets of ancient trees.
Each step taken, softly guided,
Through realms of beauty, we've decided.

In this twilight glow, fear subsides,
With every twinkling light, love abides.
A journey crafted from shared minds,
As the heart in harmony finds.

Here on this road, dreams can chase,
Every turn a brand new space.
With laughter's echo, shadows fade,
In the night, our fears unmade.

Take my hand, let's wander far,
Under the glow of a wishing star.
For in these paths, our spirits soar,
Illuminated forevermore.

Celestial Hues

In gardens lush, where colors blend,
Celestial hues, the earth's own friend.
Petals brushing against the sky,
A vibrant canvas where dreams lie.

Each bloom is touched by light divine,
As nature dances in perfect line.
From violet dusk to sunrise's gold,
Stories of beauty waiting to unfold.

Soft whispers from the flowers say,
In colors bright, we find our way.
Every shade, a heartbeat's song,
In this symphony, we all belong.

Let the sunset paint the night,
With brushstrokes soft, and pure delight.
In the twilight's arms, we close our eyes,
Awakened by the dreamer's skies.

So gather 'round, let spirits fuse,
In this world of celestial hues.
Together we'll weave a tapestry,
Of love and light, eternally.

Whispers of the Celestial

Beneath the velvet sky so deep,
Stars weave secrets that they keep.
In twilight's hush, the cosmos sighs,
Echoes of dreams in starry ties.

Softly glows the moonlit glow,
Silent stories, whispers flow.
Galaxies dance in cosmic grace,
Infinite wonders, a vast embrace.

Celestial paths of silver light,
Guide the lost through the night.
With every wish upon a star,
Hearts connect, no matter how far.

In the stillness, heartbeats thrum,
A harmony where stars come.
Whispers weave in cosmic songs,
Uniting all where love belongs.

In the tapestry of night we dwell,
Under the stars' enchanting spell.
In soft embrace of cosmic air,
We find our peace, our souls laid bare.

Dawn's Embrace

A gentle light begins to spread,
Casting dreams from night to bed.
Colors rise, the sky ablaze,
Morning whispers soft praise.

Birds serenade the waking morn,
Nature's symphony reborn.
Golden rays through leaves cascade,
In dawn's embrace, the world is made.

Each dewdrop clings to life's allure,
A fleeting moment, pure and sure.
Hope awakens in the light,
Chasing shadows from the night.

As sunbeams dance on fields of green,
The day unfolds, a vivid scene.
A canvas bright, with hues anew,
Embraced by sun, the world breaks through.

With every dawn, a fresh start calls,
A whispered promise that enthralls.
In every ray, a chance to see,
Life's beauty wrapped in harmony.

The Gilded Reverie

In dreams adorned with golden threads,
Whispers linger where the heart treads.
Imagined worlds begin to bloom,
Painting joy in every room.

The sun dips low, a fiery hue,
As twilight dances, bold and true.
A reverie where wishes soar,
In gilded realms, forevermore.

Laughter echoes, sweet and bright,
In the embrace of soft twilight.
Illusions weave in fading light,
Guiding souls into the night.

Mirth and magic intertwine,
In enchanted moments, so divine.
Crafting dreams with a gentle hand,
In this gilded, timeless land.

With every heartbeat, visions gleam,
A tranquil lull, a woven dream.
Step into wonder, let it be,
In the arms of sweet reverie.

Kindling the Night

Stars awaken, gentle and bright,
Kindling whispers in the night.
A tapestry of dreams unfolds,
In the quiet, stories told.

Moonlight dances on silver streams,
Cradling hopes and midnight dreams.
With every breath, the night does sigh,
As shadows blend with starlit sky.

Fires flicker, warm and soft,
Casting flickering moments aloft.
In the stillness, hearts align,
Kindled spirits, pure and divine.

Night's embrace, a soothing balm,
Whispers of peace, gentle and calm.
In the glow of the crescent's light,
We find solace, lost in night.

As dawn approaches, dreams will fade,
Yet in the heart, memories laid.
Kindling the night, we find our way,
In the warmth of night's soft play.

Celestial Harmony

Stars dance softly in the night,
Moonlight weaves a silver thread.
Waves of silence take their flight,
In the cosmos, dreams are bred.

Shooting stars ignite the mind,
Galaxies whisper tales of old.
In vastness, truth is often blind,
Yet in darkness, light turns bold.

Planets spin in gentle grace,
Orbits chart a quiet song.
In this boundless, endless space,
Harmony, where all belong.

Constellations sketch the past,
Through their forms, we find our way.
In each heartbeat, wonders cast,
Celestial night, our bright array.

Awake to the cosmic flow,
In the stillness, feel the cheer.
Each moment's gift, a chance to grow,
Celestial harmony is near.

Vibrant Whispers

Leaves flutter softly in the breeze,
Nature's secrets hush and sway.
Colors blend with tender ease,
In the garden, night meets day.

Birds chirp melodies so sweet,
A symphony of sights and sounds.
In this vibrant world, we meet,
Harmony in joy abounds.

Flowers bloom, their petals wide,
Painting landscapes with pure heart.
In their fragrance, peace should bide,
Every blossom plays a part.

Rivers flow with laughter clear,
Mountains rise in steadfast grace.
Whispers echo, drawing near,
In nature's arms, we find our place.

With every step, our spirits lift,
Held by whispers full of cheer.
In vibrant hues, the world's a gift,
Every moment pure and dear.

Ripples of Radiance

Gentle waves caress the shore,
Underneath the sun's warm glow.
Ripples dance, forevermore,
In their motion, spirits flow.

Light reflects on waters clear,
Softly shimmering, a dream.
As the day fades, we draw near,
To the whispers of the stream.

In the quiet, we can find,
Echoes of the universe.
Radiance in heart and mind,
Every moment a sweet verse.

Sparkling stars ignite the night,
In the dark, their secrets gleam.
A tapestry of pure light,
Weaves together every dream.

Radiance flows in every soul,
Like a river, never still.
In this dance, we feel the whole,
Ripples of a tranquil thrill.

Embrace the Glimmer

In a world of endless chase,
Find the moments, small and bright.
In each smile, a warm embrace,
Glimmers dance in soft twilight.

Follow shadows, let them guide,
Paths of light that lead us home.
In our hearts, the stars abide,
In their glow, we freely roam.

Life's a spark, a fleeting dream,
In the stillness, truth is found.
Hold the glimmer, let it beam,
Trust the whispers; hear the sound.

Underneath the boundless sky,
We are threads in cosmic seams.
With each breath, let spirits fly,
Embrace the glimmer of dreams.

In the night, let wishes soar,
Every heartbeat writes a rhyme.
Glimmers linger, evermore,
Embrace the light; it's our time.

In Search of Morning

The dawn breaks soft and clear,
Whispers of light draw near.
Shadows fade, the stars take flight,
Hope awakens with the light.

Birds begin to greet the day,
In the sky, they dance and play.
Golden rays kiss the dewy grass,
Moments of peace, they swiftly pass.

A gentle breeze stirs the leaves,
Nature's song, the heart believes.
Each heartbeat syncs with the dawn,
In search of morning, we move on.

Colors blend, a canvas bright,
Life ignited, pure delight.
With every hue, new dreams arise,
In this moment, we touch the skies.

As the sun climbs high and bold,
Stories of the day unfold.
In search of morning, spirits soar,
A promise kept, forevermore.

Dazzling Silhouettes

In the twilight, shadows play,
Figures dance at end of day.
Against the sky, they twist and bend,
Silhouettes that never end.

A silent night, the stars collide,
In harmony, they will confide.
Whispers of dreams, lost in the haze,
Captured in the moonlit gaze.

The world slips into a trance,
Each shadow takes a bold chance.
Dazzling forms in shades of gray,
Painting whispers of the day.

With every heartbeat, feelings glide,
Echoes of an evening tide.
Dazzling silhouettes come alive,
In their rhythm, we will thrive.

Underneath the calm celestial light,
Dancing dreams take fearless flight.
In this moment, lost in time,
We find our peace in silent rhyme.

Cascades of Illumination

In a garden, shadows play,
Radiance blooms in bright array.
Colors burst, sweet scents ignite,
Cascades of illumination delight.

Raindrops glisten on each petal,
Nature's wonder, we can't settle.
Sunbeams weave through leafy space,
With every glimmer, nature's grace.

Falling leaves, a golden swirl,
In the wind, their colors twirl.
Each moment reflects a spark,
Illuminating shadows dark.

A gentle brook sings its tune,
Beneath the watchful, glowing moon.
In the silence, beauty flows,
Where the heart of nature glows.

With every dawn, a fresh embrace,
Cascades of light, a warm trace.
In this dance, our spirits rise,
Illumination fills the skies.

The Luminous Voyage

Across the sea, the stars ignite,
A pathway drawn in silver light.
Waves whisper tales of distant lands,
The luminous voyage gently stands.

A vessel sails on endless swells,
Carried forth by ocean's spells.
With open hearts, we chase the night,
Guided by the twinkling light.

Moonlit waves, a soft caress,
Each ripple holds a world to bless.
Dreams take flight on breezes warm,
In this journey, we transform.

Through horizons vast and wide,
We seek the treasures that abide.
The luminous voyage unfolds so clear,
Echoes of adventure drawing near.

With every dawn, new paths emerge,
In every heart, a vibrant surge.
Together on this endless sea,
The luminous voyage sets us free.

Diaphanous Dreams

Whispers float through silver night,
Veils of mist catch soft starlight.
In the quiet, secrets gleam,
Cradled gently in a dream.

Echoes dance on gentle breeze,
Looping through the swaying trees.
Every sigh a tale untold,
In the shimmer, hearts unfold.

Clouds like feathers drift away,
Carrying hopes of a new day.
In the realm where shadows play,
We will chase the dawn's soft ray.

Through the layers, visions rise,
Painting colors in the skies.
With every breath, we take the leap,
Into a world where souls can seep.

As the morning light ascends,
Glistening gently, time transcends.
In the diaphanous embrace,
We find solace in this space.

Radiance Unleashed

Sunlight spills like molten gold,
Filling hearts with tales of old.
Each ray a thread, woven tight,
Binding spirits in the light.

Dancing shadows, playful glee,
Every moment wild and free.
Nature sings in vibrant hues,
Filling souls with morning's muse.

With every dawn, a canvas bright,
Radiant colors, pure delight.
Whirls of warmth paint the skies,
Inviting dreams to rise and fly.

In the glow, we shed our fears,
Finding joy that reappears.
Hands outstretched to greet the sun,
In this light, we are as one.

As the day begins to fade,
Memories through the twilight wade.
In the radiance, we feel blessed,
In the glow, our souls find rest.

Luminous Horizons

Where the sky meets the endless sea,
New beginnings call to me.
Golden rays on waves will play,
Painting dreams at break of day.

Each horizon filled with grace,
Whispers soft in night's embrace.
Carried forth by breezes light,
Every moment feels just right.

Chasing glimpses of what's true,
In the dawn, we find our view.
Across the waves, the light will beam,
A symphony of hope and dream.

Footprints left on sandy shore,
Stories untold, wanting more.
Luminous paths will guide our way,
Inviting hearts to always stay.

As the twilight softly gleams,
We will share our deepest dreams.
Together we'll face the unknown,
With luminous horizons shown.

Light Beneath the Canopy

Underneath the leafy green,
Nature's whispers, calm and serene.
Sunlight filters, soft and bright,
Creating patterns of pure light.

Dappled shadows play and chase,
In every corner, a secret space.
Rustling leaves sing a soothing song,
Where all of our hearts belong.

Softly stepping, hearts aligned,
In the forest, peace we find.
Every breath a hymn of grace,
In each moment, a warm embrace.

Golden rays break through the trees,
Bringing warmth on gentle breeze.
In the quiet, magic reigns,
In this world where love remains.

As we wander, hand in hand,
In the light, we'll take our stand.
Beneath the canopy, bold and true,
The path of light will lead us through.

Glimmer Beneath the Canopy

In shadows deep where whispers sigh,
A world alights as day goes by.
Leaves flicker gold in the softest breeze,
Nature's beauty brings hearts at ease.

Flecks of light through branches play,
Dancing softly, a bright ballet.
With every rustle, a secret shared,
In moments cherished, love declared.

Mossy carpets cradle each step,
Footprints lost where silence wept.
The serene touch of earthy ground,
In this embrace, true peace is found.

As twilight descends, the glow unfolds,
Stars appear, their tales retold.
Among the boughs where dreams ignite,
Hope is born in the cloak of night.

So wander deep where wonders sing,
Let your heart take flight on wing.
For under the canopy, life unveils,
A glimmering magic that never fails.

Reflections in Radiant Waters

A tranquil lake that holds the skies,
Mirrors dreams and whispered sighs.
Each ripple tells a story clear,
Of silent hopes and gentle fear.

Sunrise paints a golden hue,
Ripples dance, a joyful crew.
Beneath the surface, treasures hide,
In soft reflections, meaning bides.

The evening falls with colors bold,
A symphony of light behold.
As twilight deepens, shadows blend,
In this stillness, hearts transcend.

Rippling echoes of life so near,
Tales of laughter and of cheer.
Each glance reveals a world anew,
In the radiant waters, truth is true.

So linger long where waters gleam,
Let your spirit drift and dream.
For in the depths of nature's art,
Reflections touch the human heart.

The Dawn of Color

With dawn's arrival, skies awake,
A palette spilled where dreams can take.
Brush strokes of pink and gold unite,
In morning's glow, the world ignites.

Petals stretch to greet the sun,
Each hue a joy, a race begun.
Fields adorned in colors bright,
Nature's canvas, pure delight.

The gentle breeze, a soft embrace,
Sings life anew in every space.
From verdant hills to azure seas,
In this morning, hearts find ease.

Butterflies dance on air so light,
In the dawn's warmth, a wondrous sight.
As golden rays weave through the trees,
The world awakes with vibrant pleas.

So let your soul in colors bloom,
In the dawn's light, there is room.
For beauty lives in every hue,
A dawn of color awaits for you.

A Symphony of Luminescence

In the night where shadows creep,
A radiant song awakens sleep.
Stars emerge, a twinkling choir,
Lighting hearts with pure desire.

Moonbeams dance on waves below,
A gentle rhythm, a soft glow.
Every flicker holds a tale,
Of dreams that soar, of hopes that sail.

The nightingale sings sweet and low,
A serenade where stars will flow.
With every note, the world aligns,
In harmony, the heart entwines.

Fireflies waltz in vibrant flight,
Little lanterns in the night.
Each spark reflects a wish so dear,
In luminescence, love draws near.

So close your eyes and let it be,
A symphony that sets you free.
For in the night's enchanting glow,
A world of dreams begins to grow.

Luminescent Chances

In the quiet of the night,
Dreams begin to take their flight.
Stars twinkle bright above,
Whispering tales of endless love.

Each moment glows with a spark,
Guiding hearts out of the dark.
Paths not taken, yet they shine,
Inviting souls to intertwine.

With open arms, we embrace fate,
Finding joy in every state.
The dawn brings colors anew,
Painting skies in vibrant hue.

Hope lingers in every breath,
Life unfolds, defying death.
Grasping chances as they bloom,
Lighting up the shadowed gloom.

In every heartbeat, light expands,
Weaving dreams with gentle hands.
Together, we shall dance and sing,
Igniting joy in everything.

Flicker of Forgotten Joys

In cornered rooms, shadows play,
Echoing laughter from yesterday.
Memories flicker, soft and bright,
Guiding us through the night.

A toy left under the bed,
Tales of childhood, quietly said.
These whispers dance on the air,
Carrying us, free from despair.

Moments lost in the haze of time,
Rise again with rhythmic rhyme.
Glimmers caught in softest rays,
Remind us of brighter days.

As heartstrings pull like a tide,
We gather the joys we've tried to hide.
In the silence, they regain their voice,
In every heartbeat, we rejoice.

Let the laughter flicker and swell,
A reminder that all is well.
In simple things, find delight,
In the dawn, reclaim the light.

A Radiant Tapestry

Threads of gold weave through the night,
Crafting tales with pure delight.
Each stitch holds a memory dear,
In every color, joy appears.

Patterns dance in vibrant hues,
Every twist brings forth new views.
Hand in hand, we weave our story,
Finding beauty in our glory.

A tapestry of laughter spun,
In shadows where the light has run.
Every moment, a vibrant thread,
Creating paths where dreams are led.

Though frayed edges may seem torn,
Every flaw, a treasure born.
Love's embrace in every seam,
Binding us in every dream.

Together, our stories blend,
A radiant journey without end.
In the fabric of time we trust,
Woven dreams, in hope we must.

Beyond the Shadowed Veil

A whisper floats beyond the haze,
Guiding us through shadowed maze.
With each step, the light grows near,
Casting away our deepest fear.

The veil lifts softly, bright as day,
Revealing paths, come what may.
In the distance, a beacon shines,
Calling forth the hearts that pine.

Through trials faced and burdens borne,
Fading darkness, hope reborn.
Every star a gentle guide,
Leading souls to the other side.

In the quiet, a promise made,
In every challenge, we've delayed.
The journey calls, we must prevail,
Together, beyond the shadowed veil.

So take my hand, we'll bravely tread,
Towards the light, where dreams are fed.
In unity, we find our way,
Together, we'll greet the day.

Emanating Echoes

Softly through the night they call,
Whispers of the past enthrall.
Echoes dance on moonlit streams,
Filling hearts with tender dreams.

Moments lost, yet still hold tight,
Flickering like stars in flight.
Each resound a memory's glow,
Guiding paths where shadows grow.

In the silence, voices blend,
A symphony that cannot end.
Feeling every fervent sigh,
In the echo, we learn to fly.

Glimmers of past joys arise,
Beneath the vast and endless skies.
As the night gives way to morn,
In each echo, love is born.

So let the echoes softly play,
In a language of yesterday.
Audible threads of time entwined,
A tapestry of heart and mind.

Radiance of Dreams

In the dawn, hopes come alive,
With colors bright, they start to thrive.
Every wish a gentle spark,
Illuminating realms of dark.

Drifting through the skies so pure,
Radiant visions, strong and sure.
Softly shining, hand in hand,
Manifesting dreams so grand.

With every heartbeat, visions shine,
A universe where dreams align.
Painting moments, bold and free,
In the light, we cease to be.

Harmonious hearts sing their tune,
Underneath the silver moon.
Radiance flows, the spirit beams,
Bathed in the warmth of dreams.

With each star their wishes soar,
Glimmers of what they wish for.
In this realm, fate takes its flight,
Guided by the dreamers' light.

Twilight's Embrace

As the sun bows down to rest,
The sky wears hues that are the best.
Softly wrapped in twilight's sigh,
Embers of day bid goodbye.

Shadows stretch across the land,
Nature holds its breath, so grand.
Whispered secrets in the air,
Twilight's touch, a gentle care.

All the stars begin to wake,
Glowing softly, make no mistake.
In this light, the world feels new,
Every shade a fading hue.

Night unfolds with velvet grace,
In its arms, we find our place.
Underneath the starlit array,
Twilight's embrace guides our way.

Moments linger as we pause,
Embraced by night, without a cause.
In the quiet, hearts will find,
Twilight's love, both gentle and kind.

Luminous Whispers

In the silence softly flows,
Luminous whispers all around.
They caress the heart's deep prose,
In the quiet, beauty found.

Gentle secrets softly shared,
With each breath, the universe cares.
Voices linger, sweet and clear,
In whispers, we draw near.

Stars aligned in perfect tune,
Holding promises of the moon.
In the night's enchanting sigh,
Luminous dreams begin to fly.

Every flicker, every gleam,
Whispers of a waking dream.
With each twinkle, hearts ignite,
In the darkness, find the light.

So listen close, for love endears,
In luminous whispers, find your peers.
Every heartbeat softly sways,
Guided by the night's gentle rays.

Veils of Gossamer Light

In dusky realms where shadows play,
Whispers of dawn chase night away.
Softly woven, threads of bright,
Veils of gossamer, pure delight.

Dreams unfurl on morning's breath,
Painting hope beyond the depths.
Colors dance with gentle grace,
Illuminating every space.

Light cascades on petals fair,
A tender touch that lifts despair.
In silence's embrace we find,
A symphony, both warm and kind.

As twilight falls, the world will sigh,
With stars unspooled in velvet sky.
Veils of wonder, spun from light,
Awakening hearts to pure delight.

In this realm of ethereal glow,
Time stands still, gentle and slow.
A dance of veils, in twilight's grace,
We find our truth in this embrace.

Heartbeats of the Universe

In silence deep, the cosmos breathes,
A rhythm marked by unseen seethes.
Galaxies whirl in endless flight,
Echoes of time, hearts full of light.

Each heartbeat rings like distant stars,
Connecting us from near to far.
Through the void, we feel the pull,
Of love that makes the universe whole.

Planets spin on paths divine,
Dancing to an ancient line.
In every pulse, a story told,
Of brave explorers, dreams of old.

From stardust born, we rise and fall,
With every beat, we heed the call.
To know we're part of something vast,
A cosmic journey, unsurpassed.

In constellations, we find our face,
Each spark a trace of our embrace.
With every moment, we align,
The universe sings, your heart and mine.

Ephemeral Glow

In fleeting hours of twilight's grace,
Glimmers dance in a tender place.
Softly whispered, secrets flow,
Captured in an ephemeral glow.

Moments fleeting, like grains of sand,
Drift through fingers, unplanned,
Yet each spark holds a tale so bright,
Bathing the world in serene light.

The moon drapes silver on the stream,
A soft caress, a gentle dream.
In the hush, we find our way,
Ephemeral magic guides the sway.

Leaves flutter down, a crisp ballet,
Nature's breath in shades of gray.
Time lingers lightly, as we know,
Beauty lies in that fleeting glow.

In every heartbeat, a chance to feel,
The wonders life has to unseal.
Embrace the now, let worries go,
For life's a dance in ephemeral glow.

When Daydreams Shine

In the quiet hush of fading light,
Daydreams flicker, taking flight.
Whispers of hope weave through the air,
Painting visions beyond compare.

Thoughts meander through fields of gold,
Stories young and tales of old.
In a world where wishes twine,
Magic stirs when daydreams shine.

Beneath the boughs, where shadows play,
Imagination leads the way.
A canvas bright, holding the flow,
Of visions wild, where dreams can grow.

Soft voices rise like winds that sing,
In their echo, the heart takes wing.
Each fleeting moment, a chance defined,
To touch the essence when daydreams shine.

Let your spirit wander free,
In this realm of fantasy.
For in our hearts, the light will twine,
Transforming dusk when daydreams shine.

A Symphony of Colors

In spring's embrace, the blossoms sing,
A tapestry of hues, they bring.
Each petal dances, bright and bold,
A canvas woven, beauty untold.

Golden rays in summer's light,
Paint the sky, a dazzling sight.
From azure blue to fiery red,
The world awakes, where dreams are bred.

As autumn leaves begin to fall,
A rustling whisper, nature's call.
In amber and in crimson tones,
The spirit of the earth atones.

Winter blankets, soft and pure,
A frosty silence, calm and sure.
While colors fade in shimmering snow,
The heart still glows with warmth below.

In every shade, a story lies,
Reflected in the twilight skies.
A symphony that sings of grace,
In every moment, every place.

Celestial Waters

Beneath the stars, the rivers flow,
Whispers of dreams in silvery glow.
The moonlight dances on the waves,
A serenade that gently saves.

In quietude, the waters sigh,
As constellations grace the sky.
Each ripple holds a thousand tales,
Of lovers lost and distant trails.

The currents pull on hearts so deep,
Where secrets lie and shadows creep.
In tranquil pools, reflections gleam,
A canvas for the night's sweet dream.

With every splash, a wish is cast,
To memories held, and moments past.
As dawn approaches, light will quench,
The magic found in twilight's drench.

Celestial waters, soft and clear,
Where time stands still and love draws near.
In waves of peace, our souls unite,
Beneath the heavens, pure delight.

Glow of Reminiscence

Amidst the shadows, memories glow,
Flickering softly, time's gentle flow.
In every whisper, echoes call,
A tapestry woven, the past enthralls.

Fragrant laughter drifts through the air,
Moments captured, forever rare.
Images dance in the mind's embrace,
Illuminated dreams, a sacred space.

The warmth of voices, familiar and sweet,
Each memory cherished, a rhythmic beat.
In fading light, we gather near,
The glow of reminiscence holds us dear.

With every heartbeat, stories unfold,
The tales of life, both timid and bold.
In corners of the heart, they reside,
Carrying whispers of joy and pride.

As dusk approaches, we take our flight,
Guided by the glow, we chase the light.
Forever etched in the fabric of time,
The glow of reminiscence, a sweet rhyme.

The Fire Within

An ember stirs, deep in the soul,
A flicker of hope, a shimmering goal.
With every challenge, it starts to blaze,
A dance of courage, in life's maze.

The storms may rage, but we will stand,
Fueled by passion, as we command.
In shadows cast, a light will show,
The fire within continues to grow.

Each trial faced, a lesson learned,
In the heart's forge, our spirit turned.
Resilience blooms, like flowers in spring,
From ashes rise, new journeys take wing.

With voices strong, we raise our song,
In unity, we all belong.
Together, bright, our flames entwine,
A beacon fierce, forever shine.

In quiet moments, we find our peace,
The fire within will never cease.
For in our hearts, we hold the spark,
Illuminating paths, lighting the dark.

Horizon's Glow

The sun dips low, a golden hue,
Whispers of light in skies so blue.
Clouds embrace the evening's grace,
A painted canvas, time's soft trace.

Shadows stretch, the day bids farewell,
In this quiet, a secret to tell.
Stars awaken, dreams take flight,
The world transforms in the fading light.

Crickets sing a soothing tune,
Under the watch of the silvery moon.
A tranquil heart, a gentle sigh,
In the twilight, the spirit can fly.

Colors blend, a magic show,
Nature's art, the horizon's glow.
Endless beauty, a sight to behold,
Stories of old, in whispers retold.

With each heartbeat, hope will thrive,
In the dusk, we come alive.
A fleeting moment, forever stays,
In the glow of the dying days.

Radiant Echoes

Through the forest, light does weave,
Whispers echo, as hearts believe.
Leaves are dancing, shadows play,
In radiant warmth, the world's ballet.

Golden rays touch the morning dew,
Nature's song, a sweet renew.
Every breath, a joyful rebirth,
Echoes linger upon the earth.

Mountains high, in splendor rise,
Kissed by sun, beneath wide skies.
Streams of silver, gently flow,
In the stillness, radiant glow.

Moments captured, in timeless grace,
Reflections dance, in nature's embrace.
Voices merge, a symphony,
In radiant echoes, we find harmony.

With every dawn, hope ignites,
In shadows lost, we chase the lights.
A world alive, in every hue,
The heart rejoices, forever true.

The Shining Hour

When twilight falls, the stars ignite,
A magic hour, pure and bright.
Moments linger, time stands still,
In gentle whispers, dreams fulfill.

Moonlit paths where shadows fade,
In this silence, fears allayed.
Hearts united, spirits soar,
A tranquil dance, forevermore.

Candles flicker in the night,
Casting warmth, a soft invite.
Stories shared, laughter flows,
In the shining hour, love grows.

Glimmers rise from deep within,
A tapestry where we begin.
Every glance, a promise made,
In this moment, never to trade.

As dawn approaches, dreams take flight,
Yet in our hearts, we hold the light.
The shining hour lingers near,
In every heartbeat, love is clear.

Dance of the Luminaries

In the sky, the stars align,
A celestial waltz, pure divine.
Planets spin in graceful arcs,
As night unveils its cosmic sparks.

Comets streak, a fleeting glance,
Under the moon, we lose our chance.
Whispers carry on the breeze,
In this dance, our spirits tease.

Galaxies twirl in vast expanse,
Infinite wonders, a timeless dance.
Light-years fade, yet we connect,
In the cosmos, we reflect.

With every heartbeat, stars align,
In playful paths, our souls entwine.
Together we weave the night's embrace,
In the universe, we find our place.

As dawn approaches, the dance recedes,
Yet in our hearts, the magic breeds.
Forever tethered to the skies,
In the dance of luminaries, love never dies.

Threads of Golden Moments

In the dawn's gentle gleam,
Threads of gold softly beam,
Whispers of life begin,
A new day treads within.

Moments dance on the breeze,
With laughter, hearts at ease,
Time weaves its subtle lace,
In this warm, cherished space.

Sunlight filters through leaves,
Each sparkle softly weaves,
Painting dreams on the ground,
In beauty we are bound.

Echoes of joy abound,
In the quiet, profound,
Each second a treasure,
Woven with love and pleasure.

As twilight starts to fade,
We recall every shade,
Threads of memories bright,
Golden moments take flight.

Fantasia of Fire and Light

In the shadows, flames dance,
A flicker, a bright glance,
Blazing trails across the night,
Fantasia of fire and light.

Whispers of warmth surround,
In this magic, we're found,
Stars twinkle, wild and free,
In this vibrant tapestry.

Colors swirl in delight,
Painting dreams in the night,
Embers rise, spirits soar,
In warmth, we yearn for more.

Heartbeat of flames ignite,
Our hopes in radiant flight,
With every bright flare,
We find solace in the air.

As dawn breaks the spell,
A new story to tell,
Fantasia fades away,
But its glow always stays.

Embracing the Last Ray

Beneath the horizon's glow,
Where the sunsets gently flow,
We gather, hearts entwined,
Embracing the last ray, aligned.

Shadows stretch, evening calls,
Silhouettes against the walls,
As the day bids goodbye,
We raise our spirits high.

Golden hues begin to blend,
In this moment, we transcend,
Holding close what we see,
A shared warmth, you and me.

Fading light whispers low,
Secrets only we know,
Each twilight carries grace,
In love's tender embrace.

As darkness wraps the sky,
We let the stars reply,
For in this quiet sway,
We cherish the last ray.

Chronicles of the Glowing Night

Underneath the silver skies,
Whispers echo, dreams arise,
Stars become our guiding light,
Chronicles of the glowing night.

Stories twinkle in the dark,
Fables sung, a gentle spark,
Each twinkling star, a tale,
In the night, we set sail.

Through the shadows, we will roam,
Finding magic far from home,
With hearts aglow in the dark,
Each memory leaves its mark.

The moonlight paints the scene,
In silver threads, a sheen,
Each breath of night we share,
In this realm, we lay bare.

As dawn begins its climb,
We treasure every rhyme,
Chronicles softly gleam,
In the night's enduring dream.

Lanterns of the Heart

In the stillness of the night,
Lanterns flicker, hearts take flight.
Whispers dance upon the breeze,
Guided by their gentle tease.

Memories glow in every hue,
Casting warmth that's brave and true.
Each flame holds a secret light,
Illuminating hopes so bright.

Carried forth on dreams and sighs,
They lead us where our longing lies.
In shadows deep, they pierce the dark,
Igniting love's enduring spark.

With every lantern, stories weave,
In their glow, we dare believe.
Together, we shall not depart,
Forever keep those lanterns heart.

Glowing Amongst the Shadows

Beneath the cloak of twilight's veil,
Softly shine where echoes dwell.
In corners where the lost reside,
Glow like stars that gently guide.

In whispered sighs and tender dreams,
A dance of light in moonlit beams.
Amongst the shadows, calm and wide,
Love's embrace shall not subside.

Through tempests fierce and waters deep,
These glowing hearts promise to keep.
Each flicker tells of battles won,
A symphony of light begun.

As night enfolds its silent throng,
We gather close, where we belong.
In the quiet, love's gentle glow,
Reveals the paths we long to know.

Twinkling in the Silence

In the hush of night's allure,
Stars above begin to stir.
Twinkling softly, secrets shared,
In silence, tender hearts declared.

Each flicker holds a whispered tale,
Of hope and dreams that shall prevail.
Gentle warmth from distant light,
Guiding souls through the night.

In stillness, love starts to bloom,
Casting out all fear and gloom.
Each star a promise, shining bright,
Illuminating paths of light.

Together, we shall dance and sway,
Beneath the moon's enchanting ray.
For in this silence, hearts ignite,
Twinkling softly, pure delight.

Serenades of Soft Light

In the twilight's tender grace,
Soft light plays in every space.
Serenades whisper through the air,
Awakening the dreams we share.

Each glow a song, so sweet and clear,
Melodies that draw us near.
In the hush, our spirits rise,
Bathed beneath the starlit skies.

With every flicker, hopes take flight,
Embraced within the arms of night.
A symphony of glowing hearts,
Playing softly, love imparts.

As shadows blend with radiant beams,
Together lost in gentle dreams.
In the serenade, we find our spark,
Woven tightly, never dark.

Milton Keynes UK
Ingram Content Group UK Ltd.
UKHW010229111224
452348UK00011B/611